For Amma

Copyright © 1989 by Nord-Süd Verlag, Mönchaltorf, Switzerland.
First published in Switzerland under the title *Eine Wasserreise*.
English translation copyright © by Rada Matija AG. North-South Books English
language edition copyright © 1989 by Rada Matija AG, 8625 Gossau ZH, Switzerland.

10   9   8   7   6   5   4   3   2   1

First published in Great Britain, Canada, Australia and New Zealand
in 1989 by North-South Books, an imprint of Rada Matija AG.
First published in the United States in 1990 by North-South Books,
an imprint of Rada Matija AG.

Library of Congress Catalog Card Number: 89-42872.

British Library Cataloguing in Publication Data is available.

THE WATER'S JOURNEY

WRITTEN AND ILLUSTRATED BY ELEONORE SCHMID

North-South Books

New York

High in the mountains tiny drops of water have been carried up by the winds from the countryside below. As the air gets colder and colder the little drops freeze and form snowflakes. The wind swirls them up and down, but gradually they fall to the earth, covering everything with a blanket of soft snow.

In the mountains, the snow stays frozen all winter. But when spring comes the sun shines a little longer and every day it gets a little bit warmer. The snow becomes heavy and starts to melt

back into water. Some of the water is soaked into the soil, but when the soil can hold no more, the water begins to move down the mountain side.

The water forces its way through the soil, around the rocks, and under the roots of the trees and plants creating a small brook. It bubbles and gurgles past fresh spring flowers and animals who come out to hunt for food in the warm sun.

Several brooks come together and become a stream. The stream rushes down the mountain side, into a smooth gorge dug by the water over millions of years. Suddenly it reaches the edge of a cliff . . .

. . . . and becomes a beautiful waterfall which pours into the lush green valley below.

The water collects at the bottom of the cliff, forming a new stream which continues to move downward. As it flows down the

valley it connects with other streams and gains even more strength. Sometimes there is so much water that the stream overflows its banks. Whatever stands in its way, branches, rocks, soil, is swept along by the force of the water.

Where the valley flattens out, the stream slows down, leaving the branches and rocks and soil behind.
Several streams come together and empty into a large lake

nestled between the hills. Along the edge of the lake are fields of grain and vegetables which get their nourishment from the cool clean water and the minerals it carries down from the mountains.

The water in the lake is cool and still and full of life.
The sun begins to disappear as dark clouds come rolling across the mountains. Quickly the boats return to shore and the animals go back to their nests.

Suddenly lightning flashes. A fierce wind begins to blow and heavy raindrops fall from the sky.

At the end of the lake there is a city. Above the high walls along the shore, people sometimes stop to watch the shimmering reflections in the water. Here, the water starts to move quickly

again, pulled by the strong current of a river flowing out from the
other side of the lake.

Beyond the city there is a reservoir, which stores drinking water for the city. Some of the water from the river feeds into the reservoir and the rest flows around it. If there is too much water in the reservoir it flows over the edge of the floodgates, back into the river.

Now the water has entered a mighty river, filled with boats of all shapes and sizes. The river slowly winds its way through another city.

The water is no longer as clean as it was when it started its journey. It's filled with dirt from the fields and valleys and with waste from the towns, cities and factories along its banks.

When the river empties out into a port, the fresh water from the river mixes with the salt water from the ocean. Here, the water is so dirty that very few fish survive.

As the tide moves in and out, day after day, the water from the mountains is gradually carried out into the open ocean.

At last, the water is near the end of its journey. When the hot sun shines down on the huge blue ocean, the water on the surface gets warmer. It slowly evaporates, becoming a fine mist, like the steam in a hot shower. The mist is carried up by the winds, high into the sky, where it will stay — until it comes back to the earth as a beautiful snowstorm or warm rain on a hot summer's day.